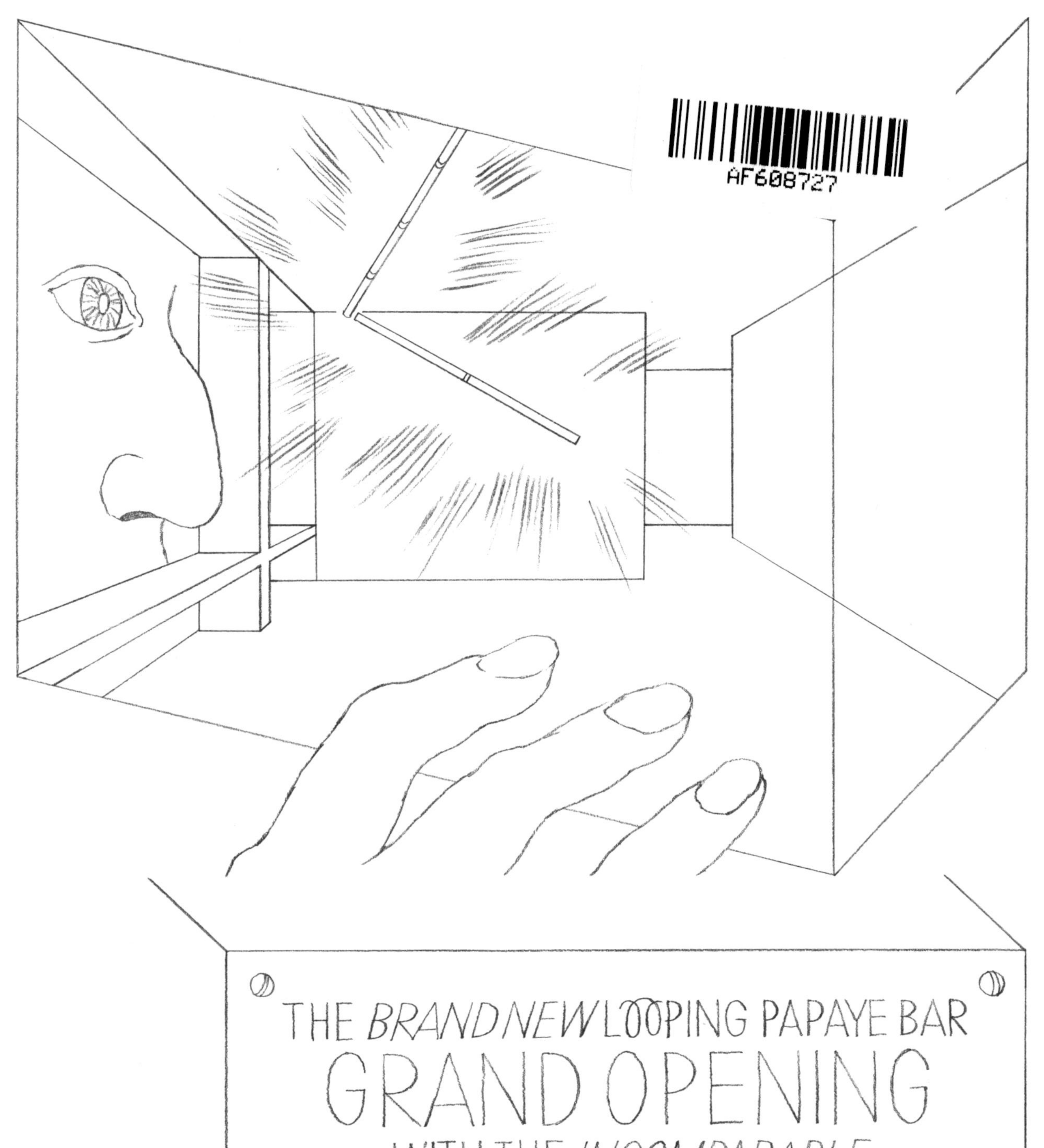

THE *BRAND NEW* LOOPING PAPAYE BAR

GRAND OPENING

WITH THE *INCOMPARABLE*

KING SALAMI SLICE

DIESEN DO. 1. DEZEMBER AB 22 UHR

LESSING 1 KREIS 2 STOCK 3

Chez Dimi, Mauro & Rafi

THE LOOPING
PAPAYE
BAR
WITH
DJ
A.C.
KUPPER
DIESEN DO.
15. DEZ.
AB 22 UHR
LOOPING PAPAYE BAR
CHEZ DIMI, MAURO & RAFI
LESSING 1 ◇ KREIS 2 ◇ STOCK 3
NÄCHSTE MAL AM 29. UND
31.12. ← SILVESTER!

THE FAMOUS LOOPING PAPAYE BAR

DIESEN DONNERSTAG
29. DEZ. AB 22 UHR
MIT DJS "DUST SURFERS"

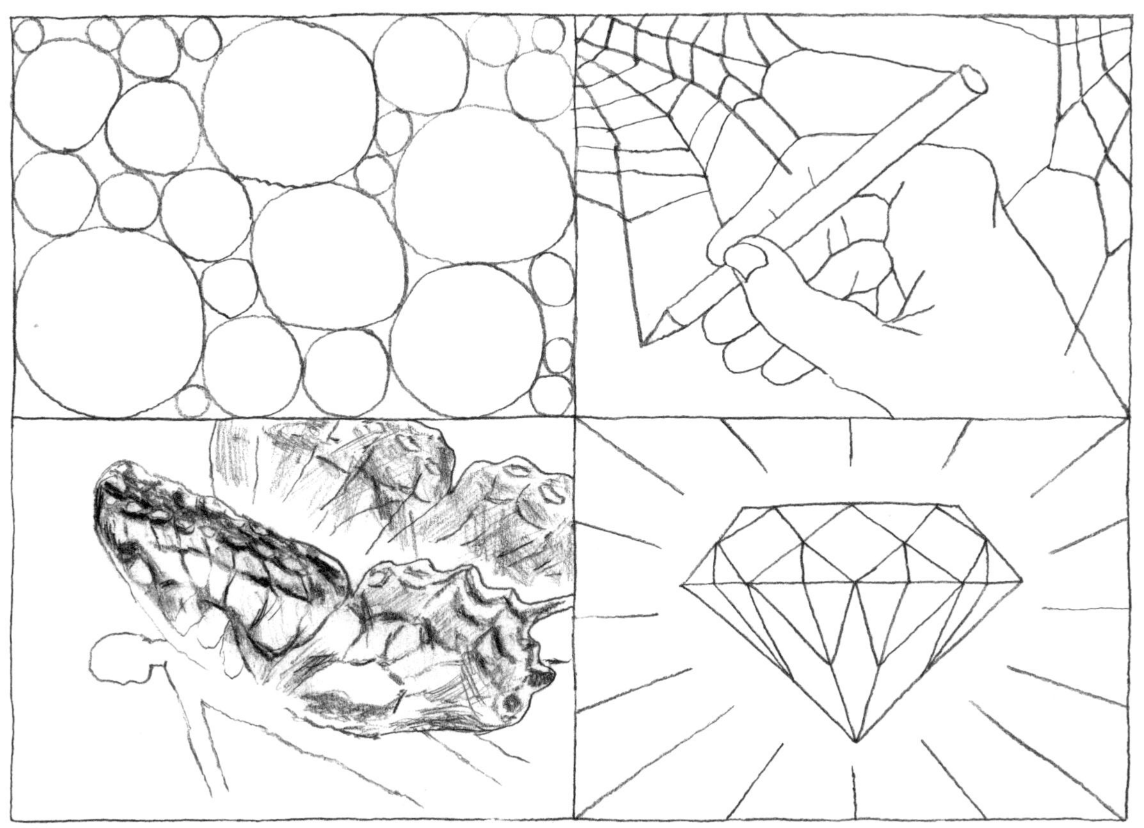

!!! SILVESTER IST ABGESAGT
BUT DOUBLE-POWER AM 29. !!!

NÄCHSTES MAL AM 12.1. UND 26.1.

THE LOOPING PAPAYE BAR
CHEZ DIMI, MAURO UND RAFI
LESSING 1 – KREIS 2 – STOCK 3

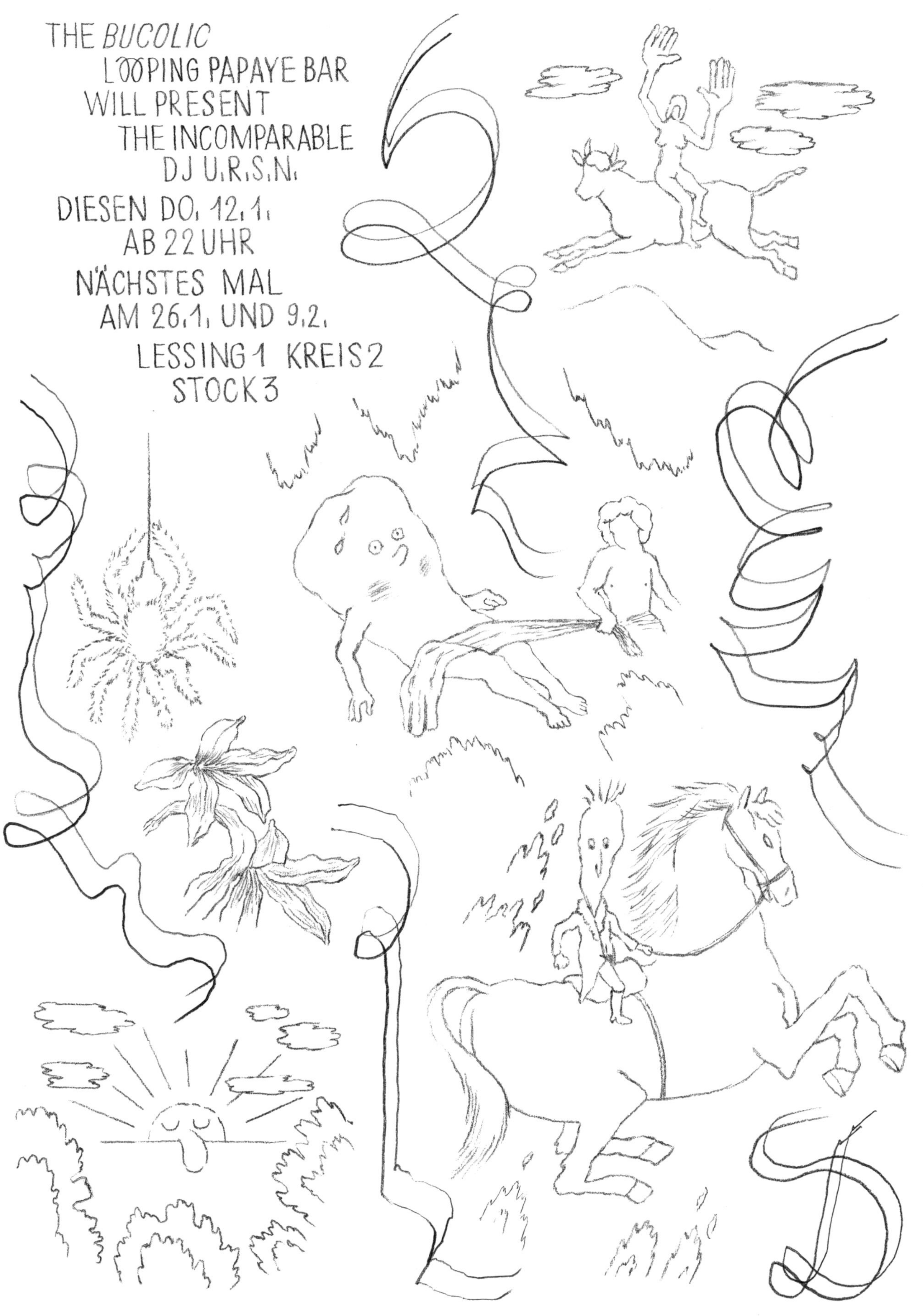
THE BUCOLIC
LOOPING PAPAYE BAR
WILL PRESENT
THE INCOMPARABLE
DJ U.R.S.N.
DIESEN DO. 12.1.
AB 22 UHR
NÄCHSTES MAL
AM 26.1. UND 9.2.
LESSING 1 KREIS 2
STOCK 3

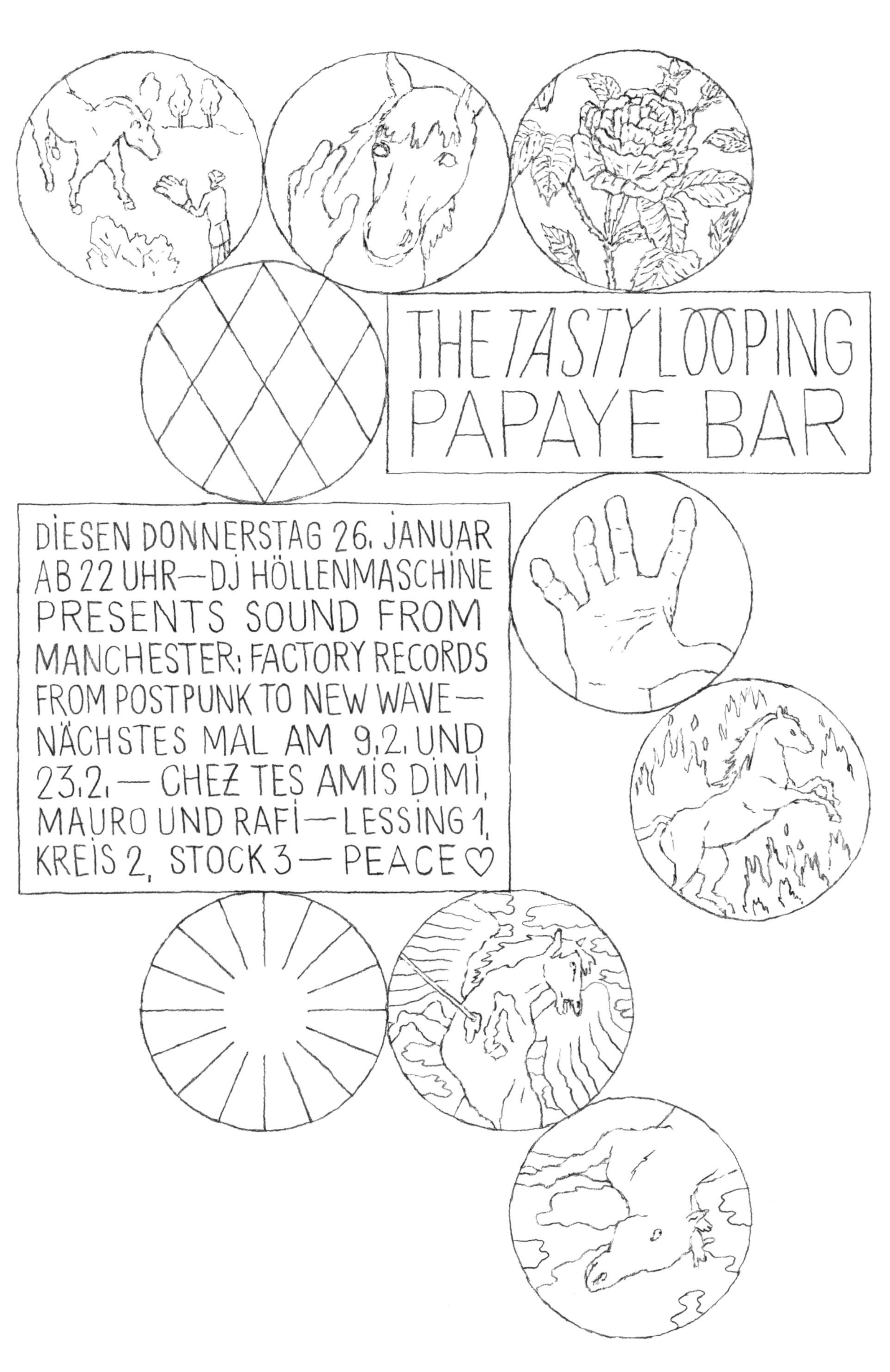
THE TASTY LOOPING
PAPAYE BAR
DIESEN DONNERSTAG 26. JANUAR
AB 22 UHR — DJ HÖLLENMASCHINE
PRESENTS SOUND FROM
MANCHESTER: FACTORY RECORDS
FROM POSTPUNK TO NEW WAVE —
NÄCHSTES MAL AM 9.2. UND
23.2. — CHEZ TES AMIS DIMI,
MAURO UND RAFI — LESSING 1,
KREIS 2, STOCK 3 — PEACE ♡

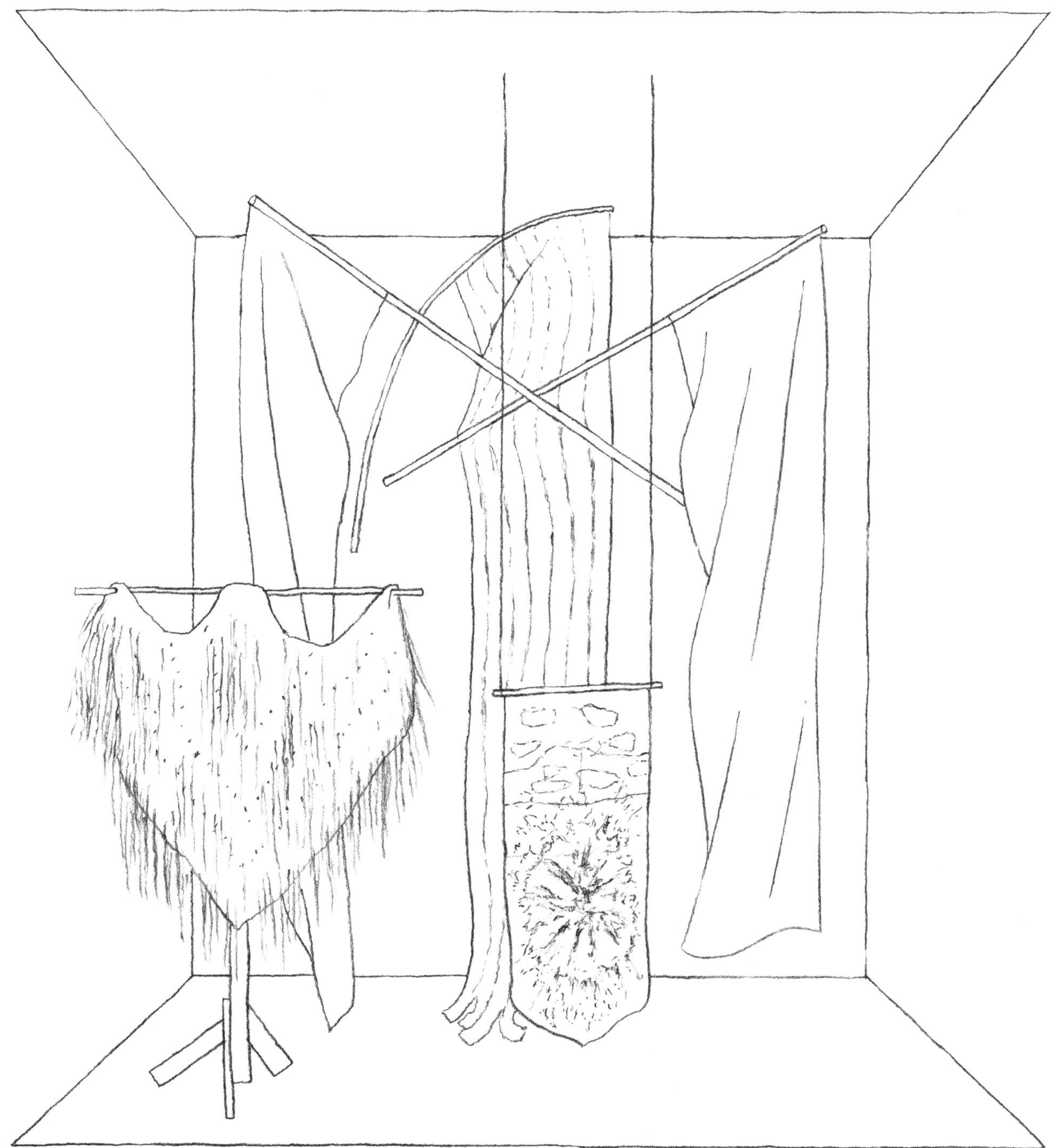

THE *GORGEOUS* LOOPING PAPAYE BAR

DIESEN DONNERSTAG 9, FEBRUAR: AFRICAN NIGHT !!!
AB 22 UHR: SINGSTREET JAM SESSION – HOSTED BY ZIMBABWEBIRD
AB 24 UHR: DJ U,R,S,N – TRANSGLOBAL SOUNDSCAPES

NÄCHSTES MAL AM 23,2, UND 8,3, — LESSING 1, KREIS 2, STOCK 3

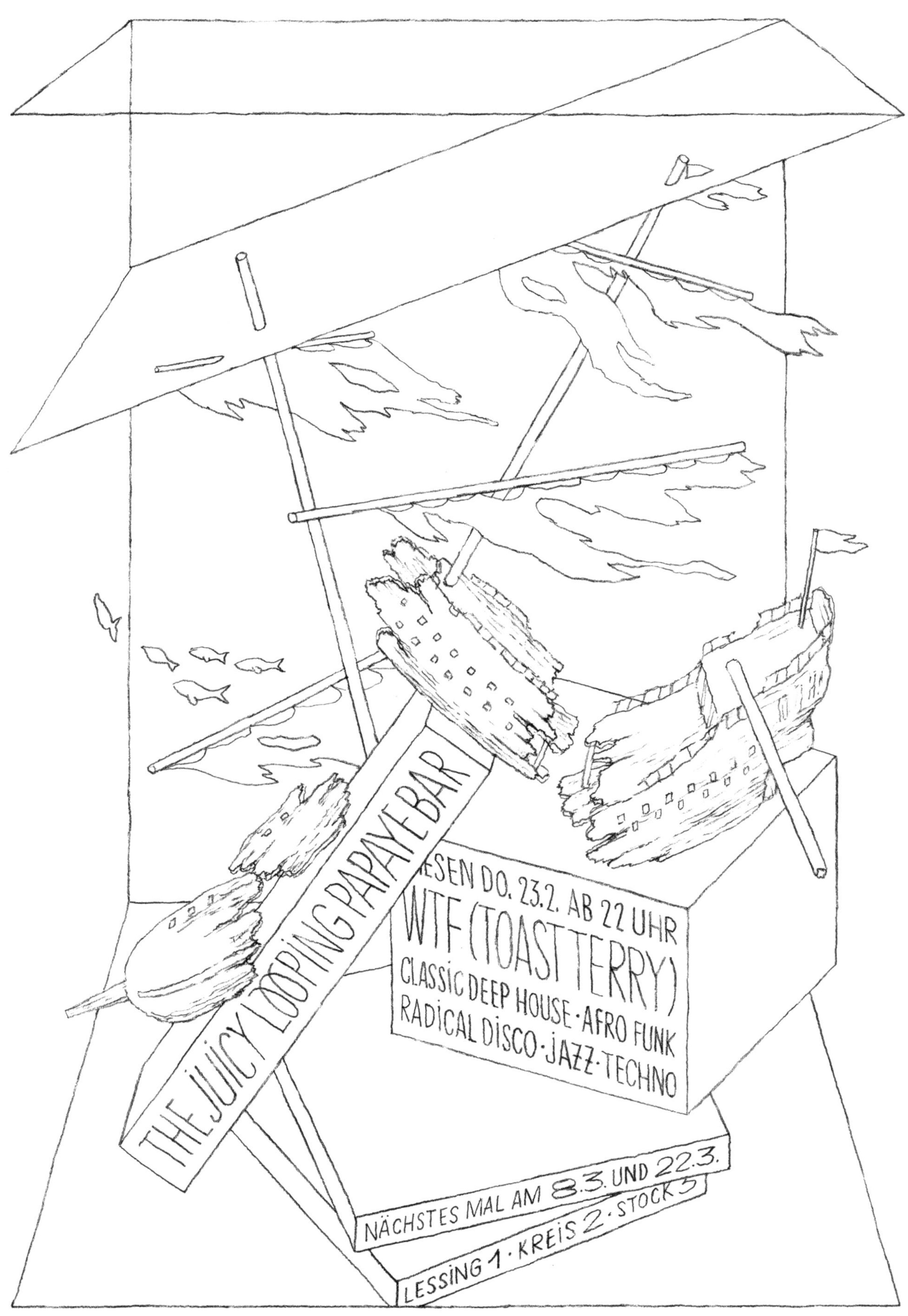
THE JUICY LOOPING PAPAYE BAR
ESEN DO. 23.2. AB 22 UHR
WTF (TOAST TERRY)
CLASSIC DEEP HOUSE · AFRO FUNK
RADICAL DISCO · JAZZ · TECHNO
NÄCHSTES MAL AM 8.3. UND 22.3.
LESSING 1 · KREIS 2 · STOCK 3

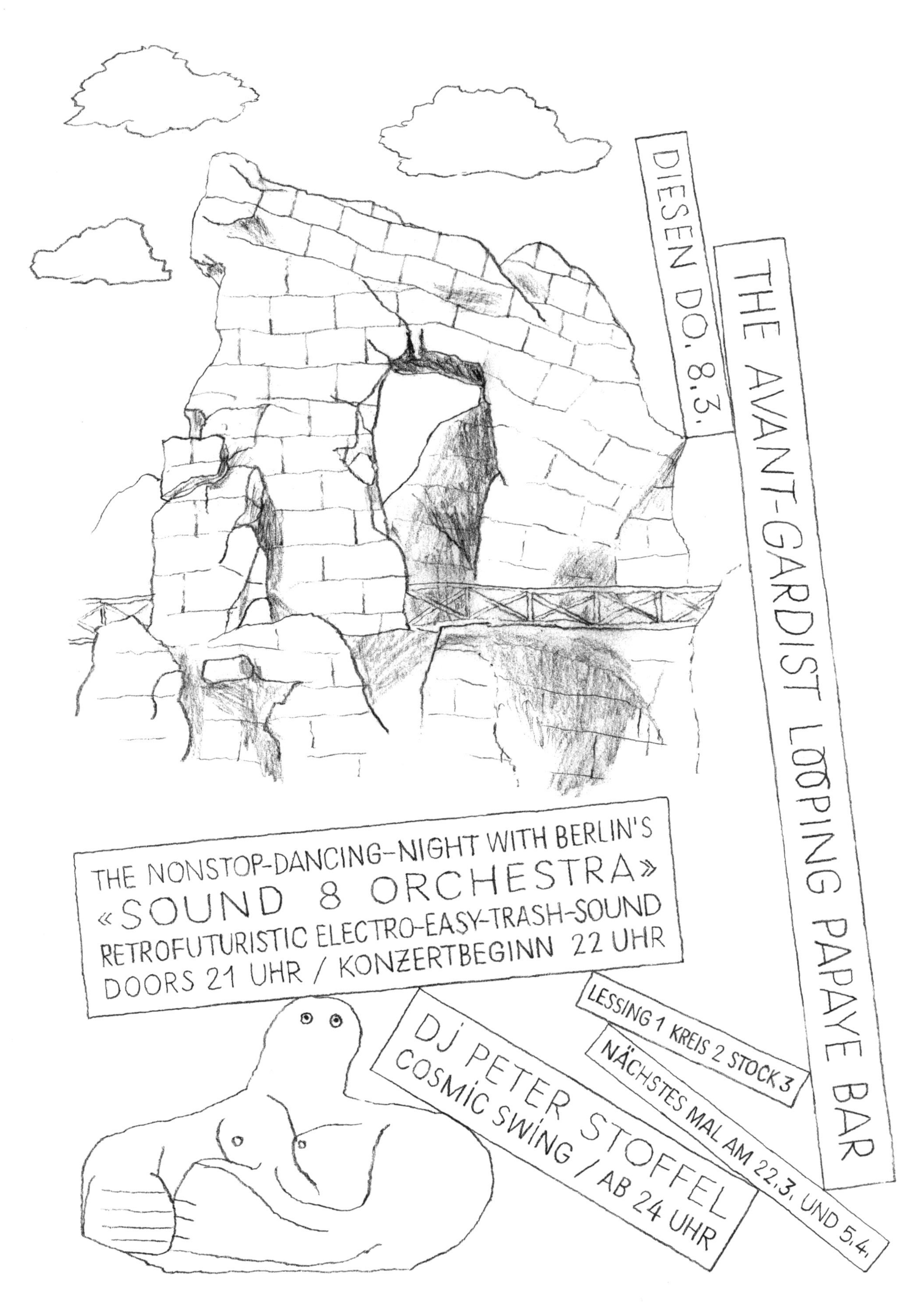
DIESEN DO. 8.3.
THE AVANT-GARDIST LOOOPING PAPAYE BAR
THE NONSTOP-DANCING-NIGHT WITH BERLIN'S
«SOUND 8 ORCHESTRA»
RETROFUTURISTIC ELECTRO-EASY-TRASH-SOUND
DOORS 21 UHR / KONZERTBEGINN 22 UHR
LESSING 1 KREIS 2 STOCK 3
NÄCHSTES MAL AM 22.3. UND 5.4.
DJ PETER STOFFEL
COSMIC SWING / AB 24 UHR

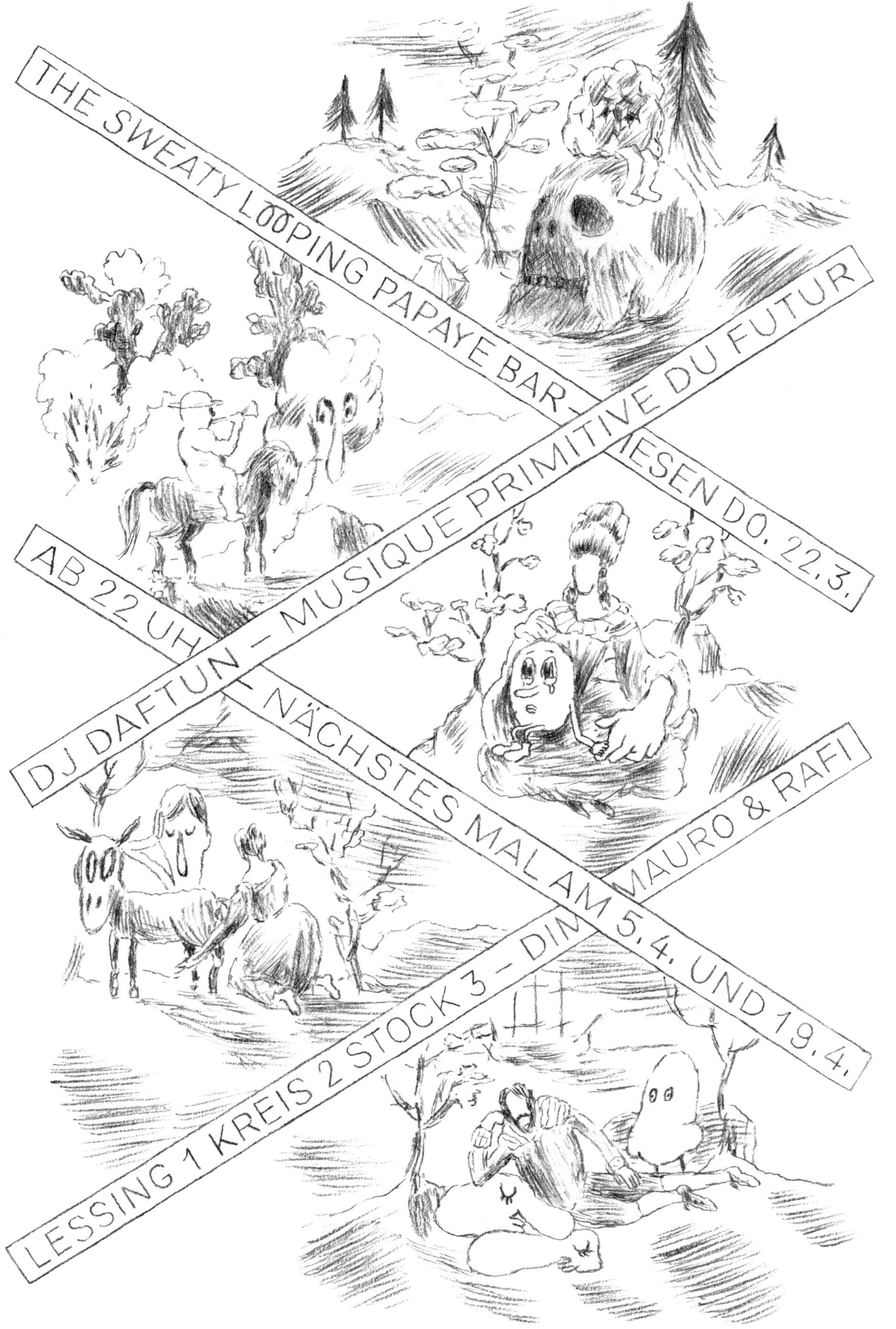
THE SWEATY LOOPING PAPAYE BAR
ESEN DO. 22.3.
DJ DAFTUN – MUSIQUE PRIMITIVE DU FUTUR
AB 22 UH
NÄCHSTES MAL AM 5.4. UND 19.4.
LESSING 1 KREIS 2 STOCK 3 – DIM
MAURO & RAFI

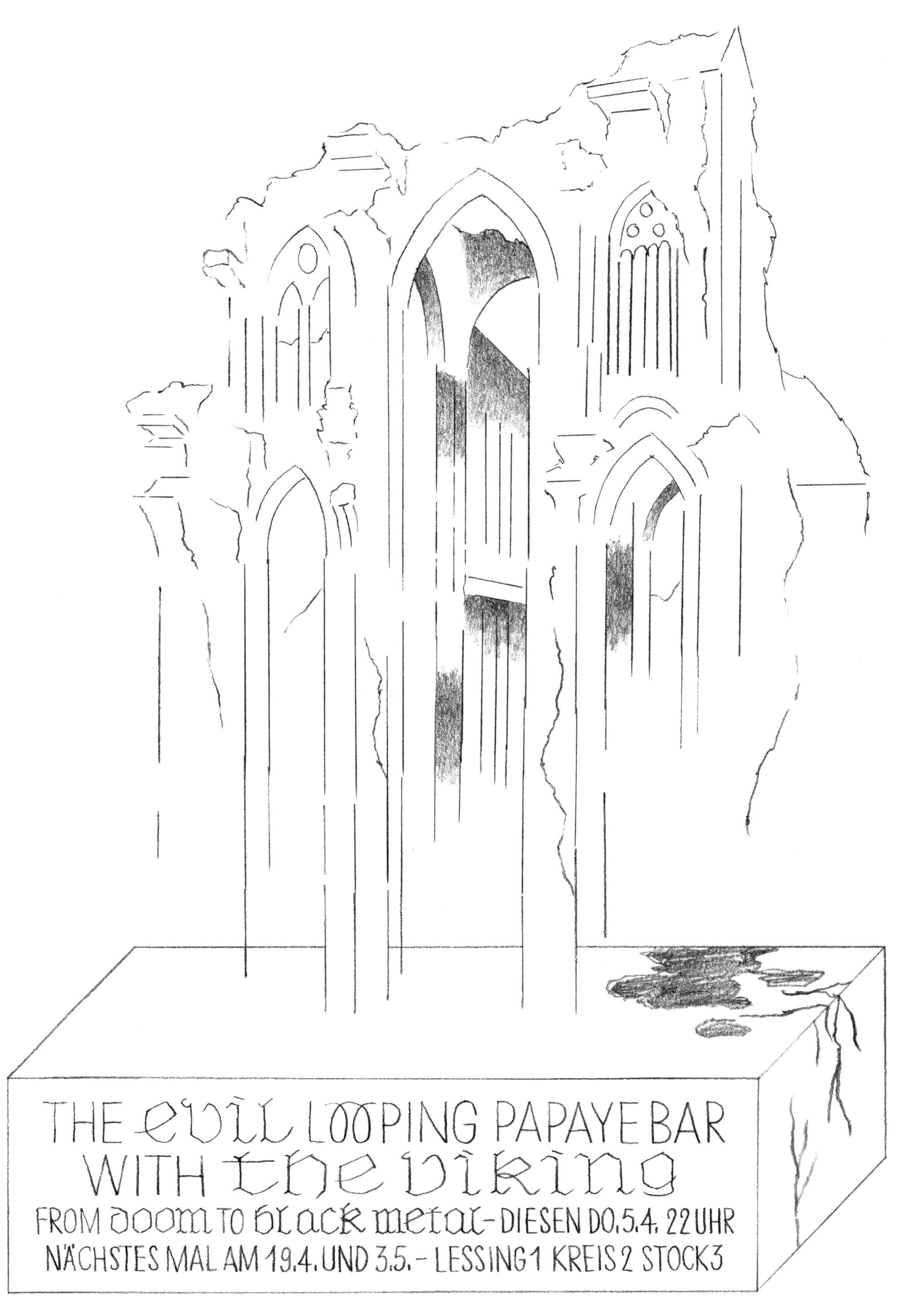

THE evil LOOPING PAPAYE BAR
WITH the viking
FROM doom TO black metal – DIESEN DO. 5.4. 22 UHR
NÄCHSTES MAL AM 19.4. UND 3.5. – LESSING 1 KREIS 2 STOCK 3

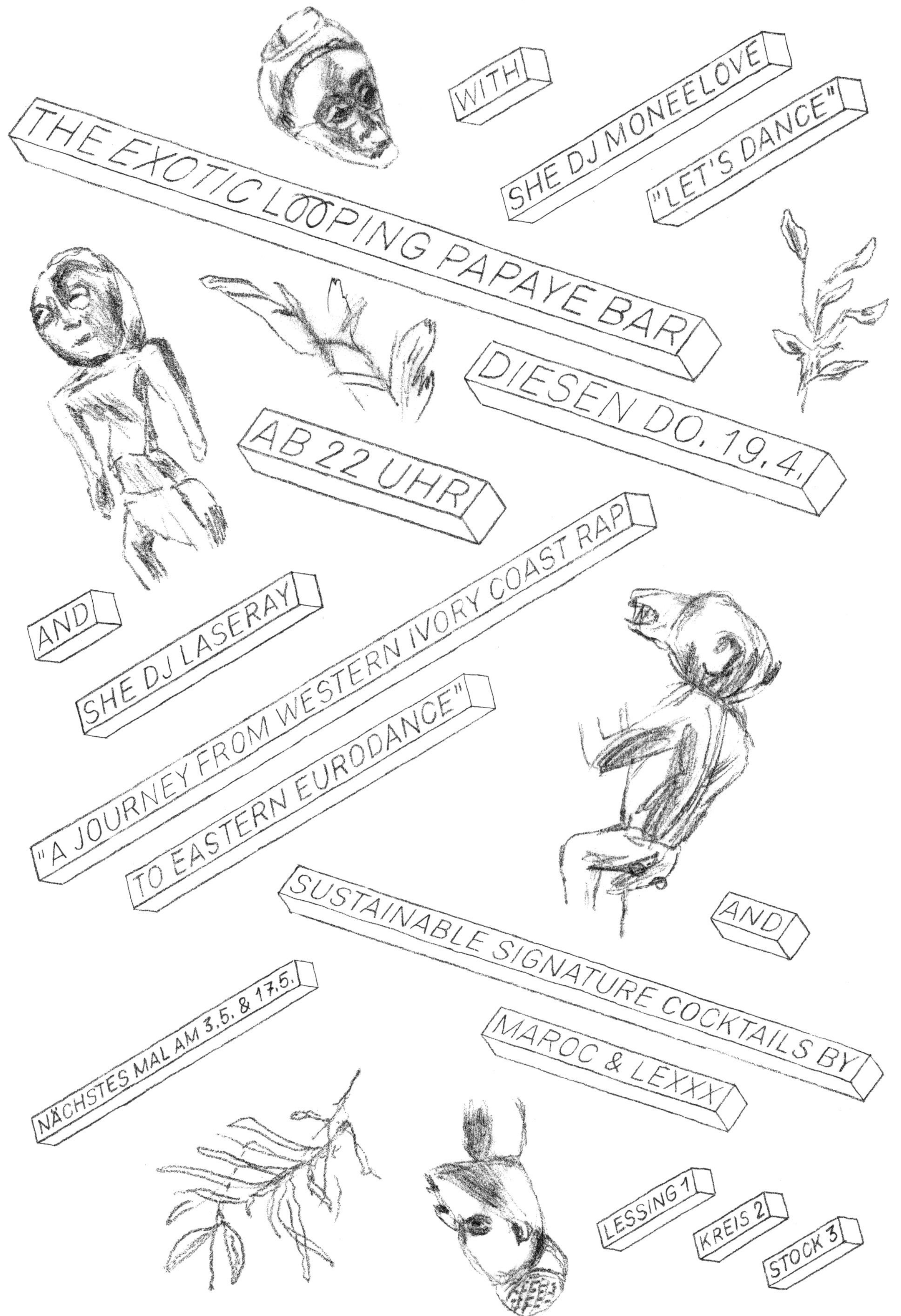
WITH
THE EXOTIC LOOPING PAPAYE BAR
SHE DJ MONEELOVE
"LET'S DANCE"
DIESEN DO. 19.4.
AB 22 UHR
AND
SHE DJ LASERAY
"A JOURNEY FROM WESTERN IVORY COAST RAP
TO EASTERN EURODANCE"
SUSTAINABLE SIGNATURE COCKTAILS BY
AND
MAROC & LEXXX
NÄCHSTES MAL AM 3.5. & 17.5.
LESSING 1
KREIS 2
STOCK 3

THE *ESO* LOOPING PAPAYE BAR

DIESEN DONNERSTAG 3.5. – AB 22 UHR

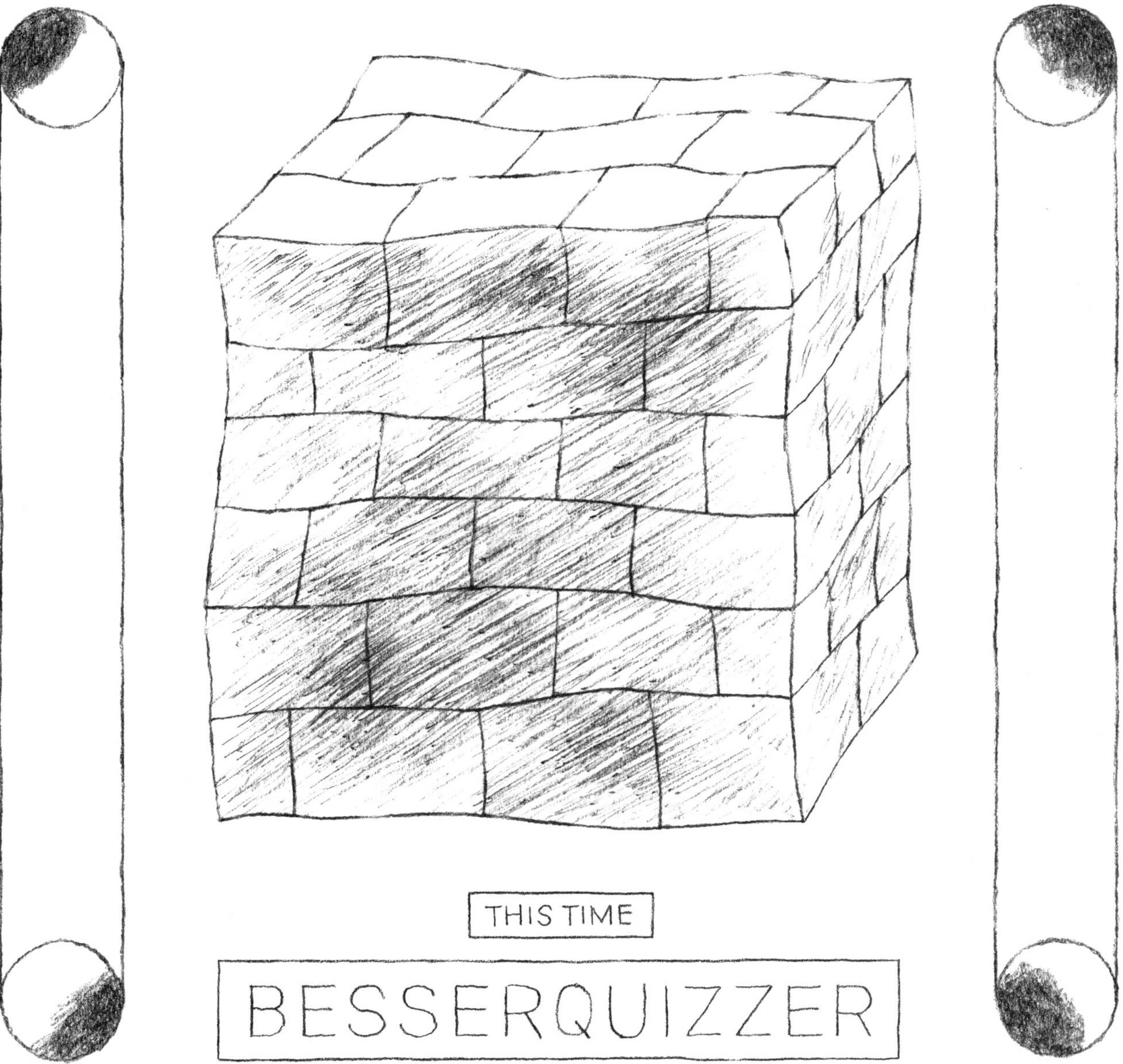

KATASTROPHALE FRAGEN –
KOMPLEXE SOUNDS MIT DJANE SUZE
UND SAKE VON SAKEO

NÄCHSTES MAL AM 17.5. UND 31.5.

♡ LESSING 1 · KREIS 2 · STOCK 3 DMR

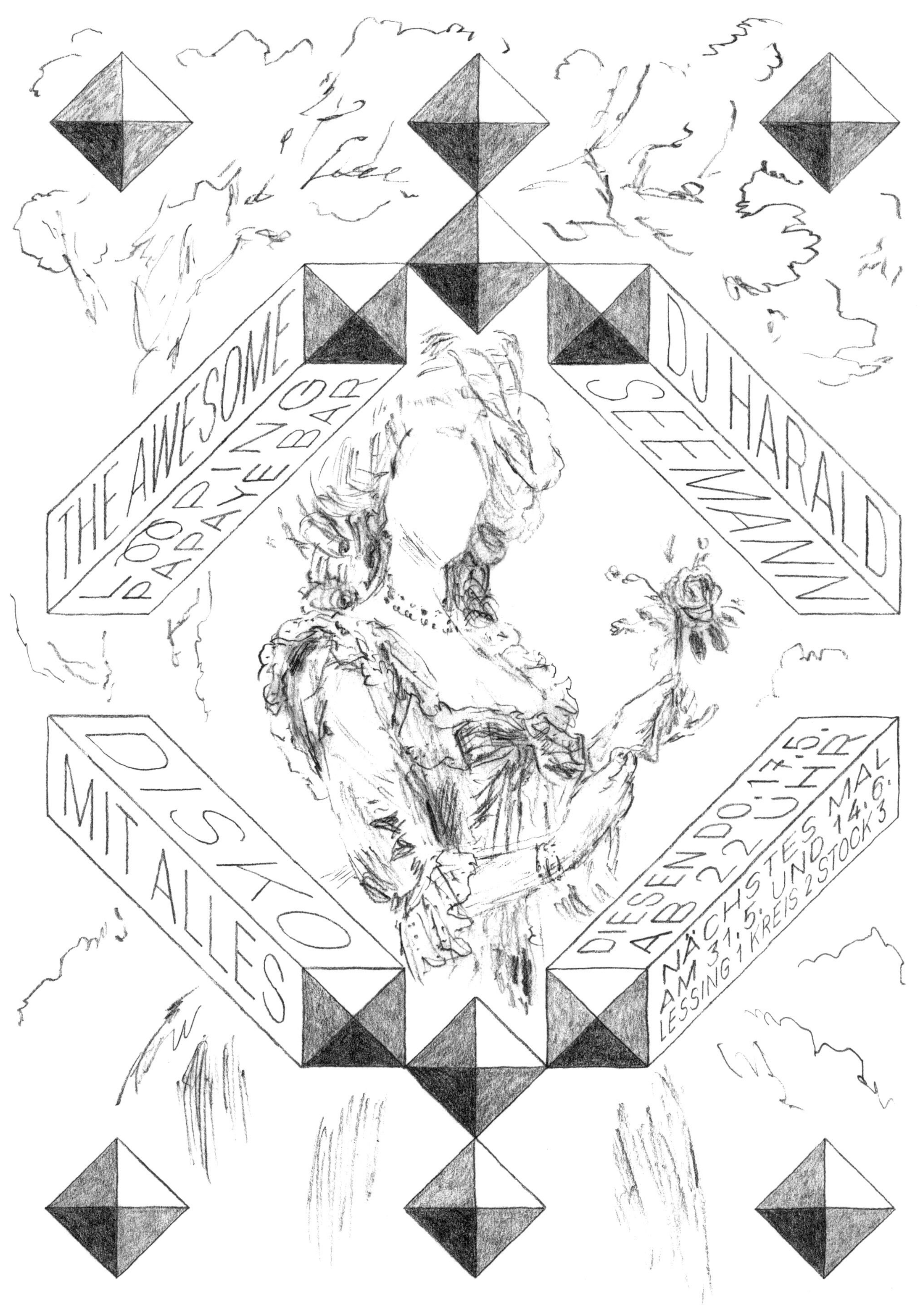
THE AWESOME
LOOPING
PAPAYE BAR
DJ HARALD
SEEMANN
DISKO
MIT ALLES
DIESEN DO. 17.5.
AB 22 UHR.
NÄCHSTES MAL
AM 31.5. UND 14.6.
LESSING 1 KREIS 2 STOCK 3

THE
MICROSCOPIC
LOOPING
PAPAYE
BAR

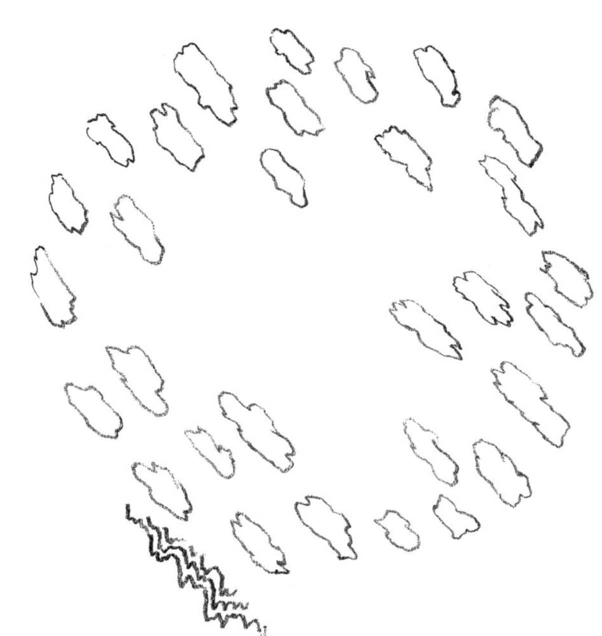

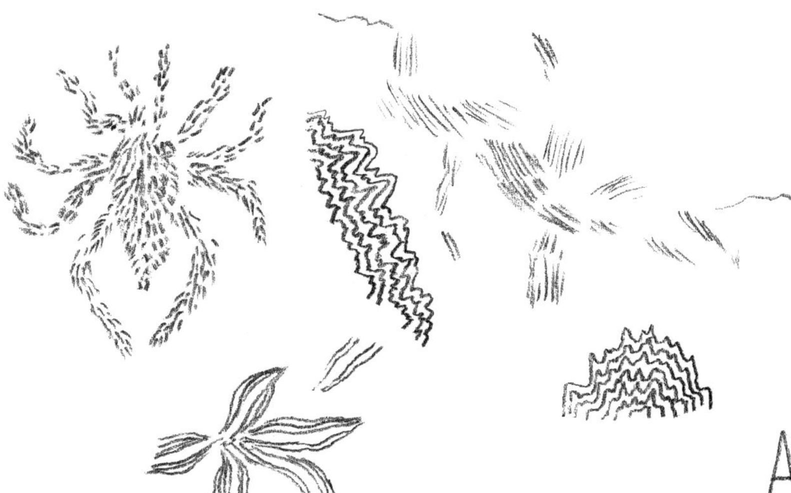

WITH
THE
GREAT
A.C. KUPPER

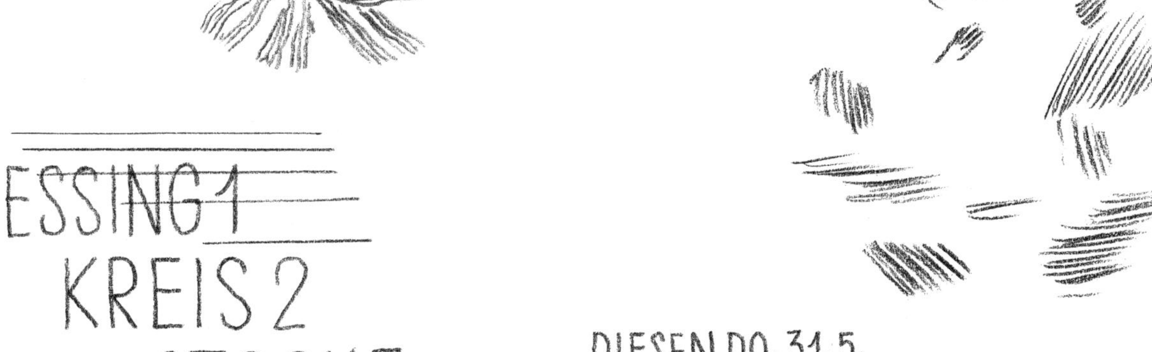

LESSING 1
KREIS 2
STOCK 3

DIESEN DO. 31.5.
AB 22 UHR
NÄCHSTES MAL
AM 14.6. UND 28.6.

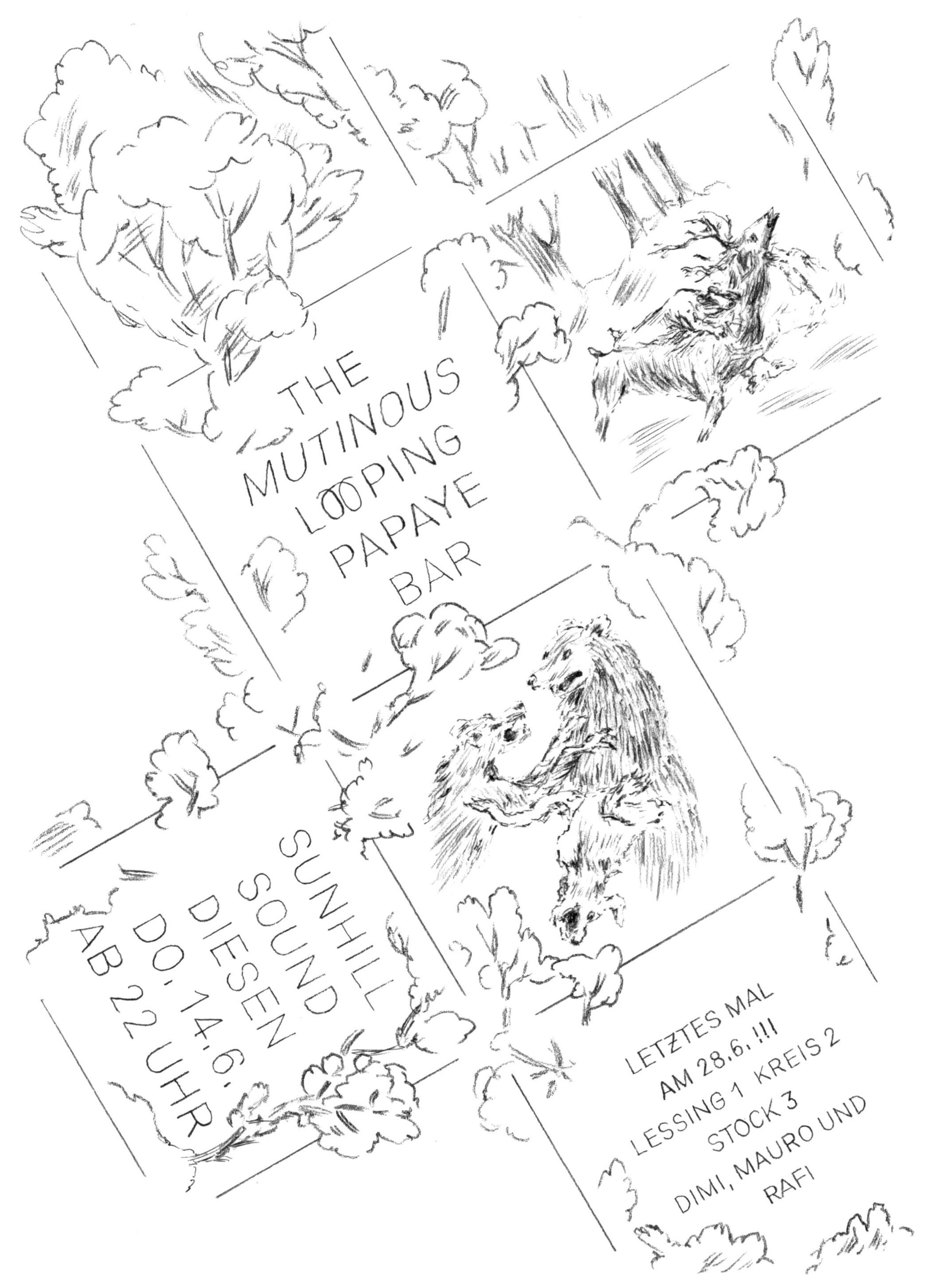
THE
MUTINOUS
LOOPING
PAPAYE
BAR
SUNHILL
SOUND
DIESEN
DO. 14.6.
AB 22 UHR
LETZTES MAL
AM 28.6. !!!
LESSING 1 KREIS 2
STOCK 3
DIMI, MAURO UND
RAFI

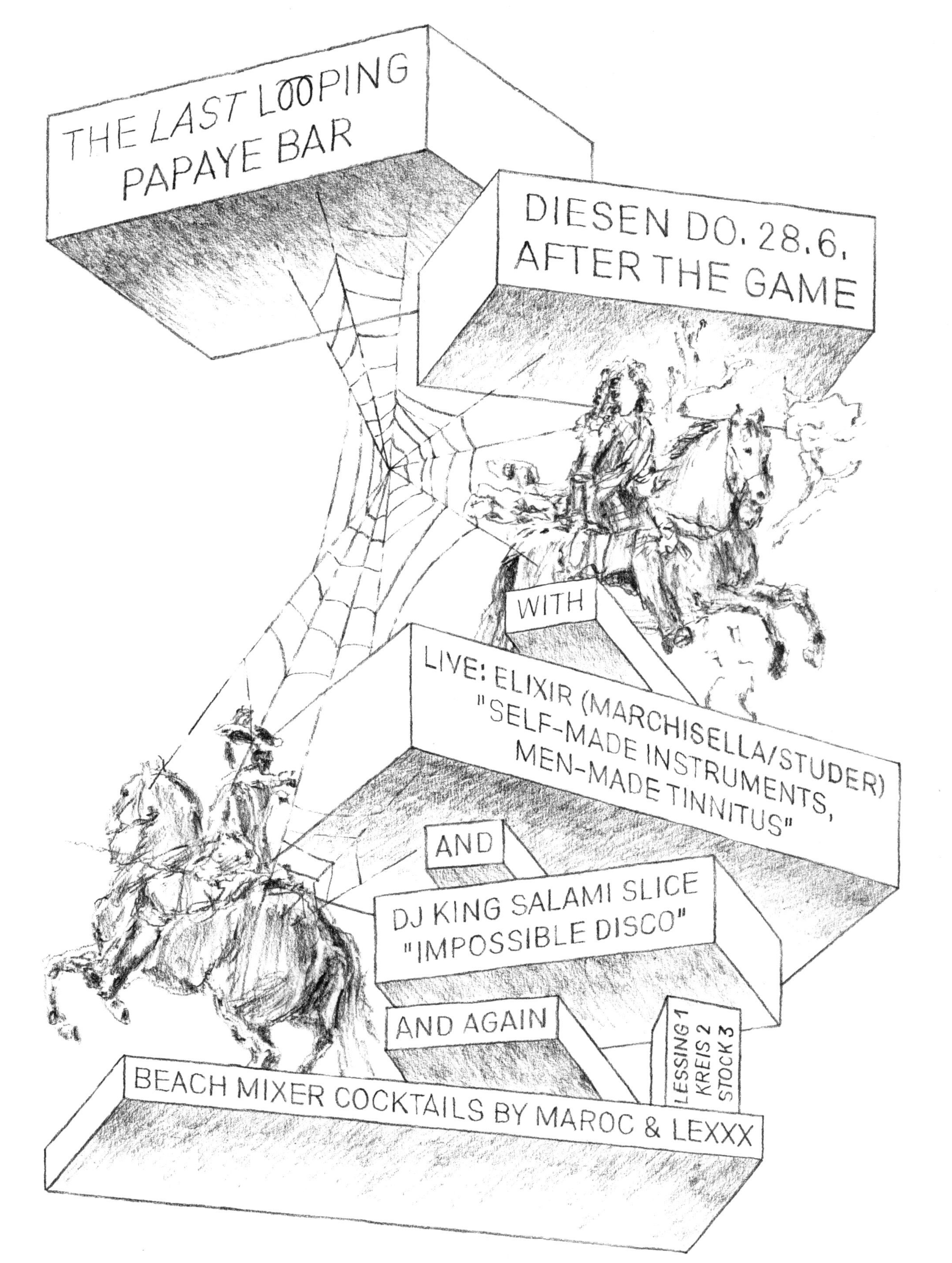
THE LAST LOOPING
PAPAYE BAR
DIESEN DO. 28.6.
AFTER THE GAME
WITH
LIVE: ELIXIR (MARCHISELLA/STUDER)
"SELF-MADE INSTRUMENTS,
MEN-MADE TINNITUS"
AND
DJ KING SALAMI SLICE
"IMPOSSIBLE DISCO"
AND AGAIN
LESSING 1
KREIS 2
STOCK 3
BEACH MIXER COCKTAILS BY MAROC & LEXXX